Love & Let Go

Love & Let Go

Reflections, Confessions,
Encouragements, and a Few
Cautionary Forewarnings from a
Father to a Daughter

PETER O'BRIEN

Library and Archives Canada Cataloguing in Publication

Title: Love & Let Go : reflections, confessions, encouragements, and a few cautionary forewarnings from a father to a daughter / Peter O'Brien.

Other titles: Love & Let Go

Names: O'Brien, Peter, 1957- author.

Identifiers: Canadiana (print) 20210243465 |
Canadiana (ebook) 20210243651 |

ISBN 9781771616041 (softcover) | ISBN 9781771616058 (PDF) | ISBN 9781771616065 (EPUB) | ISBN 9781771616072 (Kindle)

Subjects: LCSH: O'Brien, Peter, 1957- | LCSH: Fathers and daughters. | LCSH: Conduct of life.

Classification: LCC HQ755.85 .O27 2021 | DDC 306.874/2—dc23

Published by Mosaic Press, Oakville, Ontario, Canada, 2022.
MOSAIC PRESS, Publishers
www.Mosaic-Press.com
Copyright © Peter O'Brien 2022

Printed and bound in Canada.

ONTARIO ARTS COUNCIL
CONSEIL DES ARTS DE L'ONTARIO
an Ontario government agency
un organisme du gouvernement de l'Ontario

Funded by the Government of Canada
Financé par le gouvernement du Canada

Canada

ONTARIO CREATES

MOSAIC PRESS
1252 Speers Road, Units 1 & 2, Oakville, Ontario, L6L 5N9
(905) 825-2130 • info@mosaic-press.com • www.mosaic-press.com

Also by Peter O'Brien

Dream Visions: The Art of Alanis Obomsawin (Perceval Press)

A Perfect Offering: Personal Stories of Trauma and Transformation (Mosaic Press), edited with Harold Heft and Suzanne Heft

The echo is where (Carbon Publishing)

Cleopatra at the Breakfast Table: Why I Studied Latin With My Teenager and How I Discovered the Daughterland (Quattro)

INNING: How the Toronto Blue Jays Inspired Us About Baseball and Life in 53 Error-Filled, Ecstatic, Epic Minutes (Carbon Publishing)

Build a Better Book Club (Macmillan), written with Harold Heft

Introduction to Literature: British, American, Canadian (Harper & Row), edited with Robert Lecker and Jack David

So To Speak: Interviews with Contemporary Canadian Writers (Véhicule)

Fatal Recurrences: New Fiction in English from Montreal (Véhicule), edited with Hugh Hood

Published Reviews of and Praise for Peter O'Brien

"Images by renowned Indigenous filmmaker and artist Alanis Obomsawin: treasured knowledge." Margaret Atwood, author of *The Handmaid's Tale* and winner of the PEN Centre USA Lifetime Achievement Award

"Love-drenched, tenderly written stories ... *A Perfect Offering* invites us to confront, and may even help us to overcome, our deepest fears." Barbara Kay, *National Post*

"This brave collection speaks to our common humanity ... It's what happens when big questions, vital questions, are let loose in the world." Camilla Gibb, author of five internationally acclaimed novels, including *Sweetness in the Belly*, adapted into a 2020 film starring Dakota Fanning

"Searing, compelling ... This emotionally honest book is simultaneously brutal, beautiful, and deeply inspiring." Jennifer Meeropol, granddaughter of Ethel and Julius Rosenberg

"This book will break your heart right open, and that's a good thing — vulnerability draws us closer." Mike Downie, Co-Founder of the Gord Downie & Chanie Wenjack Fund

"I would like to thank Peter O'Brien ... I am blessed for his experience, his intelligence, and his commitment to always learning. I am better because of him." Melinda Harrison, multi-year All American in five swimming events, Olympian, and author of *Personal Next*

"Engaging and articulate, like listening to a first-class baseball announcer. Wonderful tidbits of trivia." W. P. Kinsella, author of *Shoeless Joe*, made into the movie *Field of Dreams*

"This book casts a warm light on a father and daughter enjoying some great times together." Gordon Lightfoot, inducted into the Songwriters Hall of Fame, his songs have been recorded by Elvis Presley, Johnny Cash, and Bob Dylan

"Delightful, clever, and downright laugh-out-loud funny. What a lucky daughter!" Linda Nielsen, author of *Between Fathers & Daughters*, and former President of the American Coalition for Fathers and Daughters

"By turns funny, insightful, and moving, O'Brien connects ancient history to contemporary family life in a fresh and thoroughly engaging way." Vicky Alvear Shecter, author of *Cleopatra Rules!* and *Warrior Queens: True Stories of Six Ancient Rebels Who Slayed History*

"... savvy irreverence ... bracing and unexpected combinations, this guide propels us down any number of dream paths we might travel ... down-to-earth approach ... chatty, accessible tone." – *The Hamilton Spectator*

"... stunning and constantly shifting ingenuity ... O'Brien's sinuous and insinuating text babbles like a brook, flows like a stream, trickles and pools like something spilled and sticky." Garry Leonard, Professor of English, Comparative Literature, and Cinema at the University of Toronto

"... interesting and informative reading. ... the interviewer / letter writer, Peter O'Brien, was well-matched with the authors ... With any

luck [*So To Speak*'s] worthiness to the average reader will be recognized."
– Marc Côté, *The Globe and Mail*

"… illuminating in an intellectual way … these interviews are fascinating and immensely valuable for their informal views they give us of creative minds at work." – George Woodcock, *Books in Canada*

"These interviews answer a modern need to add document to creation – a form of oral history … into writers, their artistic experiments, their strivings, sincerities, postures and endeavours." – Leon Edel, winner of the National Book Award and the Pulitzer Prize

"*So To Speak* has something for every reader: human interest, political comment, the creative process, and more. … Peter O'Brien manages to avoid ivory-tower irrelevance." – *Quill & Quire*

"… electricity, banter, stimulation – call it what you will …" – *Westender*

"This is a collection of intriguing, some very good, writing, questioning themes and realities that escape the city limits. This breaking of borders seems to me a great and powerful advantage." – Alberto Manguel, *NOW*, Officer of the *Ordre des Arts et des Lettres* of France, and the former Director of the National Library of Argentina

What thou lovest well remains,
                              the rest is dross
What thou lov'st well shall not be reft from thee
What thou lov'st well is thy true heritage

~ Ezra Pound

For Siobhan,

heading out on a grand new adventure

Contents

Preface

Love & Let Go offers a few words of advice and encouragement (and perhaps even some insight) for my daughter as she heads out on her own.

It gives me the opportunity to say a few things to her that I otherwise am too awkward, burdened, or nervous to say to her directly. It has a few spots of fatherly observation and some teachable moments, but I hope it's not too paternalistic. I would rather my daughter see moments of love and respect for what she has become and what she has the potential to achieve in the years to come.

She can read these brief essays randomly, at her own leisure. She may even find a few thoughts and reflections that help her with questions and doubts that we all have. If these words have some resonance for her as she learns to stretch her wings, as she begins this new chapter of her life, I'll be pleased.

I never had similar words from either of my parents when I left home and headed out on my own – first to college and then into the working world. My father died when I was still an infant, and my mother, who brought up her own 10 children and then 12 stepchildren, simply never had the time or inclination to relay snippets of wisdom or advice that I might benefit from as I developed my independence.

There is nothing extraordinary in the ideas within these pages. My daughter and I share the same dreams, inadequacies, doubts, and ambitions as many others do.

What is unique is the time that my daughter and I have spent together, and that can never be replicated or reconstructed – or celebrated too much, as far as I am concerned.

Each of us has to find our own path, even if we later discover that similar paths have been trod by multitudes of others. It is in navigating our own path in our own incomparable and singular way that we shape who we are, how we learn, and what we achieve.

Connecting these two ways of seeing – realizing that in the grand scheme of things we are (in all our ordinariness) part of a much larger picture, and yet appreciating the special within ourselves and those closest to us – determines in large part how happy we are and how we define this happiness.

Love & Let Go allows me to remember some adventures my daughter and I have had together, and to present some wisdom that she might find of interest or use.

For these joys I will never be able to thank her enough, but this book is a start.

Beginnings and Endings

"What we call the beginning is often the end," says the poet T. S. Eliot.

You are now beginning the next phase of your life: Saying good-bye to familiar parts of your life as you head out on grand new adventures, moving toward your own personal independence. Some good-byes will be permanent (including high school friends you'll no longer see) and some will be partial (family support that was once all-inclusive begins to fade as you become more self-reliant). Each of these good-byes, and many others, are essential to the process of growing and maturing.

The world is equal parts creation and destruction, joy and sadness, wisdom and ignorance. That may seem like a harsh way to see things, but I don't think it is. New flowers and plants grow best in soil that is saturated with the decaying richness of other flowers and plants. New emotions and sensitivities flourish on the foundations of earlier, perhaps less mature emotions and sensitivities.

When you were a small girl you would ask me: "How many more days until I'm going to be four years old?" You would wonder: "Dad, what does pineapple taste like?" You would remind me of our shared adventures: "Remember when we went to the zoo last summer and I got to ride on a camel!"

Each moment is part of the fast-running and impassioned river of time in which we find ourselves. Perhaps it is only within this tumult of constant change – the rushing moments fading and disappearing if we don't make conscious efforts to hold on to them – that we are able to find ourselves.

Sometimes it is possible to capture the significance of those ephemeral moments as they pass by, to understand how the fleeting fragments are connected, and to appreciate the many beginnings and endings that we all live through. Some poets can do this. Some scientists can, and some parents. All children can, because for them the world is continuously new, and constantly changing.

A Mobius strip (a surface that has only one side), here masquerading as the symbol for infinity.

By connecting the beginnings and endings of the small components of our life, the smiles and the tears, we can make out the larger arc of our lives. For you, finishing grade school, and then middle school, and now high school, becomes a way to mark the steps of your education, to know that there is continuity to your learning, to appreciate that you are moving forward, with the potential for new insights, observations, and experiences always in front of you.

This ending of your childhood is the beginning of a new chapter – the new book – of your independence.

I know you are feeling a bit apprehensive about this next part of your life, this path before you that is still not very well defined. I know you are filled with questions, and that there will be many new questions in the coming days and years.

But you would never be here, at the beginning of this new odyssey, if you were not able to say good-bye to the things and the thoughts that got you here. You don't have to disregard them completely, but you do have to say good-bye to them, and then fold their lessons and learnings within you.

"The end is where we start from," says Eliot.

A Daughter-Shaped Space

Poet and novelist Margaret Atwood talks about the many ways a father can occupy or consume the space surrounding his daughter: "Encouraging, malignant or violent, benign and loving, maddening or boring, or simply looming large through their absence – for every daughter there is a father-shaped space that somehow must be dealt with, however well or badly it may have been filled."

I know that I have not always given you the space to be the person you were becoming. Fathers are good at some things, but they can be dim and dumb about many things. When you were a young child I remember people asking questions of you: "What grade are you in now?"; "What are you doing over the summer?"; "Where did you get those cute pink boots?" I would sometimes chime in with the answer, not allowing you the opportunity to answer the question.

There were other times when you wanted more attention from me, and I was unable to appreciate that, or to supply it. And there were times, as you were discovering your own self and perhaps wanting less attention from me, when I was oblivious to your desired liberties.

I also know that I have embarrassed you many times. That is one of the things that fathers and mothers do almost effortlessly. (I still vividly remember that my mother once kissed me in front of my fellow Grade 4 students – it remains one of the most mortifying experiences of my life.)

Most parents do not set out to embarrass their children. Perhaps it's more accurate to say that children, desirous of asserting and celebrating their independence, are embarrassed by parents holding on just a bit tighter than the child is comfortable with. As children get older, they want more freedom … and that's just when parents want to hang on longer.

Although the Lebanese poet and philosopher Kahlil Gibran is not as topical these days, when I was a teenager he was constantly invoked. I was the valedictorian at my high school (an "honor" not for having the highest marks, but rather voted on by my fellow students) and in my parting speech I quoted Gibran: "Your children are not your children. / They are the sons and daughters of Life's longing for itself."

It can be hard for parents, for fathers, to fully grasp the burgeoning separateness that their children are continuously forming. Although I am my mother's son, I am also my own sovereign self, however long it has taken me to realize that. You likewise are my daughter and yet you are your own sovereign self. These can be tough lessons to learn – both as children separate themselves from parents, and as parents try to separate themselves from their children.

I hope that in the midst of my own ego, insecurity, and selfishness, I have given you some opportunity to craft your own place in the world. And that I've allowed you the freedom to carve out – with whatever tools you've been able to find, make, or invent – your own daughter-shaped space.

A drawing you did when you were 10 years old. I've always thought that these were pretty good likenesses. I may take up a bit more space in this drawing than you do, but you come first.

4

Presence and Absence

In your first few years of school, we would often walk down the street together, hand in hand.

It was one of my greatest pleasures: Simply walking down the street with you, talking about your friends, your teachers, the weather, or whatever  adventures we were planning for the coming days. Our hands were always in motion … slightly swinging and swinging slightly … back and forth. Our hands were softly connected as we talked about all the things that drifted through our thoughts and our imaginings.

Cicero, the great Roman orator and a devoted father to his beloved daughter Tullia, said: "What has nature wanted to be more pleasurable to us, what has nature wanted to be more dear to us, than our daughters." I agree.

Your wrists were often adorned with a few bracelets that you had made. Sometimes I also wore one of your woven "friendship bracelets."

"Tell me what colors you'd like for your friendship bracelet, Dad, and I'll make one just for you," you'd say. "How about green and purple? I think those would be good colors for you."

Often you had painted your fingernails – sometimes each nail a different color – and I would watch the bright colors sparkle as we walked.

You would instinctively hold my hand a bit tighter when we were crossing the street, or when we came upon a crowd of unfamiliar people, and you wanted that extra bit of comfort and reassurance.

When you started going to high school, this hand holding started to change ever so slightly, at first. As you developed your growing independence, you didn't have the need to hold hands quite so often. Sometimes I would tease you or make an animated gesture that demonstrated we should still be holding hands, and you would offer your grudging hand, or gently remove it from mine – as though this small gesture was a way to demonstrate your burgeoning freedom and self-reliance.

By the end of high school, we no longer walked down the street holding hands. You seemed especially concerned that one of your friends might see you holding hands with your father. And of course, I would tease: "Just imagine, Sweets, if someone – one of your friends perhaps! – saw us holding hands! And that you had a father! How mortifying would that be!?"

As you now head out on your own, we won't have many opportunities to walk down the street together, holding hands or not.

I'm hoping that, eventually, when we are both older, we might be able to recapture that simple pleasure. Maybe then you'll feel our hand-holding connection is not for support or reassurance, but rather as one of the most elemental ways for two people to connect. Maybe we'll recapture that simple joy when you have your own kids and realize what a transporting delight it is to walk down the street with your child, hand in hand.

Whenever the time comes, I will be ready for it and will enjoy it – there beside you as we walk together, our connected hands swinging slightly and slightly swinging.

Your Natural Talents

You often asked me – over a meal, as we're out walking, or just going about our daily rituals at home – what courses you should be taking at school, or whether you should wear this shirt or that shirt, or whether you should play this song or that song at your next recital. These decisions seem monumental sometimes, even if they quickly fade from importance.

I've always said the same things in response to your questions: "I'm not sure"; "Do what you think is best"; "What do your instincts tell you?"

Usually, I never do know the best course of action. I try to push the decision back to you, so that you

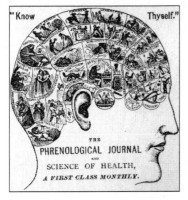

Navigating the best way forward from the many opportunities that present themselves – an early Phrenology diagram.

learn to decide for yourself, and constantly feel the process of making up your own mind. If the decision is as small as what socks you should wear that day, or if it's as large as what college you should attend or what your first job should be, I still think it is best that the decision come from and through you.

I am always amazed – in the midst of various competing interests, and surrounded by many nebulous possibilities clouding the decision – that you figure out the best course of action for that particular decision at that particular time.

In his world-shaking book *On the Origin of Species by Means of Natural Selection, or the Preservation of Favoured Races in the Struggle for Life* (I love the beauty of the full title), Charles Darwin talks about how throughout the natural world, there are a multitude of "exquisite" and "beautiful adaptations" that lead to "good and distinct species" in the "struggle for existence," a phrase which he uses, he says, "in a large and metaphoric sense."

We all struggle, says Darwin. We all have "infinitely complex relations" with the things around us and with the seasons through which we live. Adaptation to our changing circumstances – varying our responses to suit the moment, accumulating experiences to make ever better decisions, learning how to decide what is the best course of action for us at the moment – is both the best and the only way forward.

Animals and insects and plants and humans are constantly adapting, continually searching out what works best. Sometimes things happen by chance, or it is just trial and error. Sometimes circumstances are beyond our immediate control. But sometimes humans can bend the world to suit their needs and their strivings.

Although you may not necessarily think of it this way, you have constantly been shaping a wide range of exquisite adaptations to your world. You have weighed options and made decisions, and then lived with the consequences of those decisions. You have navigated infinitely complex issues – and it has been beautiful for me to watch.

It is always a great and comforting pleasure for me to say to you: "Fantastic recital! I loved it!" and "Wow, you really did great on your math test" and "They have been giving you more and more responsibility at your job – that proves they really trust you."

Continue to trust your instincts, to make up your own mind, to pay attention to the multitude of possibilities around you. That is the best way to evolve and to adapt to the changing opportunities that await you in the coming years and decades.

The Single Smile Effect

You may have heard of the "butterfly effect." It helps interpret massive weather patterns, but it also illustrates other parts of our personal and collective histories.

Coined by scientist Edward Norton Lorenz, the "butterfly effect" explains how massive changes in weather can begin by inconsequential occurrences: For example, a hurricane that might have found its genesis in the flap of a butterfly's wing several weeks earlier.

This idea of small events having the potential for cascading, far-reaching effects – perhaps years, decades or centuries from now – is not so strange or inconceivable. I would say each of our lives is full of them. Although many people (our family included) can only trace their family lineage back a few generations, each of our lives has been dependent on a dizzying array of random and sometimes chaotic past acts. Here's what I mean.

Five thousand years ago a mosquito buzzing in the ears may have kept a couple awake a few extra moments, which may have led to them enjoying some fleeting amorous comforts, which may have led to the birth of a child, who may have been one of our distant, distant relatives.

Five hundred years ago a bit of rotting meat could have become home to some nasty little bugs, which may have found their way into the meal of one of our distant family members, sending them off to an early grave and snuffing out all future trace of that branch of the family.

And what of the microorganism known as *phytophthora infestans*, responsible for the Irish potato famine of the mid-1800s, which is why many of our predecessors immigrated to North America?

These specific events, microscopic or otherwise, were never recorded, but in our own family there is a relatively recent event that helps illustrate what I'm getting at. My maternal grandmother wrote about a traumatic event in her childhood that changed the course of her life, and therefore of my life, and of your life. When she was 12 years old her father and two brothers, William, 19, and Thomas, 21, were driving to the local county fair in a farm wagon, when they were struck by a passing train. Her two brothers died instantly. "This was a mental shock from which my mother never fully recovered," she writes. As a result, her parents (your great-great-grandparents) sold the farm, animals, and machinery, and moved to the local town. That is where she later met her future husband (your great-grandfather), which has led, to state the obvious, to you and me being alive.

 Our personal histories are teeming and overflowing with these sorts of random events: A mosquito, a bit of rotten meat, a destructive microorganism, a passing train.

All of this makes me think about how each of us has a multitude of ways that we can affect those around us. Often we'll never know (in fact, we cannot know) the affect we're having.

A single smile, a few words of encouragement, a moment out of our life to help someone else – these can have long-term, fantastically influential affects on those around us.

Perhaps a teacher encourages the study of math or art in an otherwise wayward student; a nurse provides a smidgen of extra attention to a patient, which can lead to a more complete recovery; a quick and spontaneous decision you take to befriend a fellow student leads to new self-confidence. Every day our lives are filled with such happenstance, such openings.

I hope that you never forget the influence the minute decisions of our passing days can have. It may begin with a single smile.

I Believe!

What distinguishes human beings is *not* that we can build monuments, or create great works of art, or come up with faith-based and scientific hypotheses to explain our world. It's that we *believe* we can do these things.

We trust our imaginations, we follow hunches, we listen to our dreams, we allow our thoughts to lead us.

We have a great belief in belief.

I sometimes question and doubt the thoughts or conclusions of others. I think we all do. For example, I am amazed that some people believe that the most important thing we can do is make lots of money, to the exclusion of so much else. I am concerned that some people spend most of their time entertaining themselves, with games or drugs or self-obsessed pursuits, which leads to the avoidance of so much else. I am bewildered that some people deny the role of science or the place of religion when contemplating inexplicable questions, all of which ends up in the ignorance of so much else.

In his great song of the self and its limitless possibilities, the poet Walt Whitman says: "Do I contradict myself? | Very well then I contradict myself, | (I am large, I contain multitudes.)" Whitman knew that each one of us has urges and ecstasies. He says that we are untranslatable, that we have beliefs, and that these beliefs help to define us and make each of us simultaneously connected to each other and unique.

When I am feeling particularly despondent about the state of the world (there are always plenty of opportunities for that) I remember that the world is large and full of contradictions – that it is able to carry on despite the sparks and conflagrations of ignorance that we each harbor. The world can absorb the vast repository of our disparate and sometimes tormented beliefs.

You too will run into people who believe all sorts of things – some sensible, some lunatic. Just remember that the world is big enough, strong enough, and welcoming enough to accommodate all these ideas, all these meanderings, all these beliefs. If you worry too much about the capricious beliefs of others, you'll drive yourself to distraction, or worse.

Many beliefs that you'll see in your fellow students and co-workers are insupportable or ill-formed or small. That's okay. Holding on to those fallible thoughts is what makes each one of us human.

I hope you appreciate that all of us have beliefs that we may not be fully able to understand or explain to ourselves. Sometimes we can direct our imaginations, and sometimes our imaginations direct us.

I guess that is a sort of belief – an understanding that we all, whether we wish it or not, are lead by or follow our beliefs. That's part of what makes us what we are.

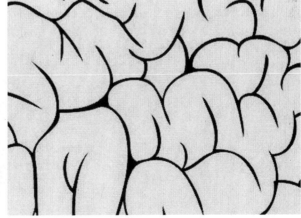

This seems to me a rather curious place to see beliefs, and the belief in beliefs, but this is the design we've been given and that we gave ourselves.

What's the Difference?

Alice Munro, that marvelous chronicler of the small and the momentous moments that influence and shape us, says in one of her stories: "Every year, when you're a child, you become a different person. Generally it's in the fall, when you re-enter school."

The same can certainly be said when going off to college, or heading out into the working world. You are about to become a different person. You remain rooted in everything you have been up to now, but as you establish your independence, you begin to focus your attentions toward your own desires, becoming more unique in your own skin, thoughts, and actions.

Perhaps becoming different only means finding what has been there all along, hidden in plain sight among your changing infantile, childish, and teenaged yearnings. All it takes is for you to see through the shifting fogs, the swirling eddies, and the many stones on the shoreline to discover what has always been.

Becoming different means that you are now able to compare yourself to others who are markedly different from you. To talk and argue and celebrate with others who are unlike you. To examine closely the memories, dreams, reflections that other people have. And then to use that knowledge to clarify your own way of seeing the world.

Becoming different means beginning to unlock the small, inevitable steps of personal change that we all experience. The moments – still not fully formed – when we come to new thoughts, new ideas, new wonderments. These changes always occur but we are not always aware of them. College and job workplaces are a good time to do some of this unlocking.

Difference is, of course, different for every person. And every one of us has brushstrokes of uniqueness, genes of peculiarity, and syllables of individuality that separate us from all others.

Your life has, of course, been different from every other life that has ever been. It's now up to you to celebrate those differences, to explore them, to put them to use.

No one will ever think of family dynamics as you will. How could they? Your familial story is different from all others.

No one will ever listen to music the way you do. How could they? Your musical knowledge has been customized by your own desires and choices over the years.

No one will ever understand science or math or philosophy or economics as you do. No one will ever think about personal responsibility exactly the way you do. How could they? If we are the sum of all that has gotten us to here and now ("I am a part of all that I have met," says the poet Tennyson, in "Ulysses," one of my all-time favorite poems) then you have connected these things in ways that no one else ever has.

You are about to become the person that everything so far has led you to. You will be wandering among things that are similar to what you know, and many that will be different. And that means lots of adventures.

The Child is Mother of the Woman

William Wordsworth wrote a marvelous little poem, "My Heart Leaps Up," that has stayed with me since I first read it in high school. In it he writes: "The Child is father of the Man," which I take to mean that the things we do and learn as a child stay with us and inform the rest of our life, and that the child is indeed wiser than the man. Children have natural wisdom and innate intelligence – things that older people would do well to remember, and recapture if they can.

You have learned so much in your childhood, and I am sure that many of your affections will follow you all the days of your life.

I remember one day, when you were five years old and in Grade 1, you came home and wanted to talk about Pablo Picasso. Your teacher at the time had been talking with you and your fellow students about Picasso's powerful anti-war painting *Guernica* as a way to connect you with the activities surrounding Armistice Day / Remembrance Day / Veterans Day (the name changes from country to country).

"We're studying Picasso in school," you told me. "Did you know he had a blue period, and then a rose period, but it was really more like a red period because he painted more with red?"

As we looked at an image of *Guernica*, our conversation took on a life of its own. You pointed out to me the anguished woman on the left side of the painting. "At first I thought that lady was holding a turtle, Dad. Now I think it's a baby. Is that her baby she's holding? Is that baby dead? That's sad."

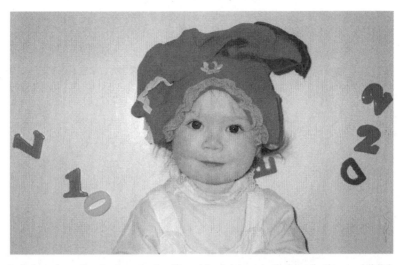

I always thought there was significant insight and wisdom in those childish eyes of yours, even when you were doing something silly, like wearing a bathing suit on your head.

We also spoke about the horse at the center of the painting – which you called a dragon – and about various other elements, including a severed hand and screaming faces.

I pointed out various things that you had not noticed, and you pointed out to me various things – including a mouse perched on a window ledge – that I had not noticed before.

I was struck by your ability to see so many things in the crowded canvas, and how you absorbed, in your own way, the pain and anguish that Picasso so evidently wanted viewers to experience.

Picasso understood this power that children have of seeing into the life of things. As he said (perhaps echoing an idea similar to that of Wordsworth's): "Every child is an artist. The problem is how to remain an artist once one grows up."

So too did the scientist Marie Curie, who won two (two!) Nobel Prizes – in Physics (1903) and in Chemistry (1911): "All my life through, the new sights of Nature made me rejoice like a child," she said. This from a woman whose work with radioactive materials means that her early papers, and even her personal cookbook, remain to this day in lead-lined boxes – that's how radioactive they still are!

The child is mother of the woman. Within his marvelously metaphoric statement, Wordsworth articulates the simple and complex power that children have. I think this youthful insight will serve you well as you get older. It can be difficult to preserve, and there will be many pressures on you to abandon such wisdom, but I do think it is possible.

Weorc, Wyrk, Work

Some of the words, from the past 1,000 years or so, and from various languages, that have helped inform and influence our word "work" – proving that a lot of, well, work went into making our word "work."

It may not be wise of me to say "work hard" – and then trust that the rest will fall into place – but that is a good place to start.

There are, of course, many things that you cannot control. You may not be able to influence the habits of your college roommates or co-workers very much, and you will not always be able to direct how others see you and your unique talents. But you can control how hard you work and therefore the range and depth of opportunities that come your way.

When you entered the 9th grade at age 13, I was impressed that you set out clear academic goals for your four years of high school. "Dad, I want to get a 92 percent average in Grade 9, a 93 in Grade 10, a 94 in Grade 11, and end off with a 95 in Grade 12."

I never, ever, have been as driven as you – arithmetically or otherwise – and the four-year plan you set for high school still inspires me.

You did, in fact, achieve your year-by-year high school goals, by following the incremental steps and the prosaic tasks necessary to get you there. You are now out on your own in part because of that sharp-eyed focus.

Gewaurki
Verk
Vorke
Wærc
Wærk
Warc
Warch
Wark
Weorc
Weorrc
Werah
Werch
Wercke
Wergo-
Werk
Werkan
Werkke
Wherk
Wircan
Wirke
Woorke
Worc
Worcke
Worke
Wourke
Wrke
Wurc
Wurch
Wurk
Wurkijan
Wurtch
Wyrcan
Wyrk

Of course there are many different ways to define work, and many different ways to define success.

Isaac Newton, arguably one of the most influential scientists and mathematicians of all time, was one of the most unassuming when it came to his own achievements. Toward the end of his life (after laying the foundation for classical mechanics and co-inventing calculus) Newton stated: "I do not know what I may appear to the world, but to myself I seem to have been only like a boy playing on the sea-shore, and diverting myself in now and then finding a smoother pebble or a prettier shell than ordinary, whilst the great ocean of truth lay all undiscovered before me."

Although Newton spent a huge amount of his working life on such misconceptions as the Apocalypse (he estimated that the world would not end until at least the year 2060) and Alchemy (he continuously researched ways to turn base metals into gold), he still had the supreme confidence to make such a humble statement at the end of his otherwise stellar career.

For you, being unassuming may not be the best work strategy right now, especially as you head out to make your own mark in the world. Sheryl Sandberg, the chief operating officer of Facebook, talks about the need for women to be confident, believe in themselves, and to work hard for what they really want. In her book *Lean In: Women, Work, and the Will to Lead*, she talks about how men often explain their success by crediting their own innate qualities and skills, while women often attribute their success to an ability to work hard.

You certainly have the ability to work hard, which like many other things in life, can be habit-forming. Now that you are surrounded by other talented people, and in a much more competitive environment, the pressures to work harder, faster, and smarter only increase. You have to work even harder in order to continue learning at the rate you've set for yourself. And that is not such a bad thing. The ramp does get steeper, but your facilities and your muscles also get stronger.

I encourage you to work hard because I have the confidence that this is exactly what you plan to do.

The Truth Must Dazzle Gradually

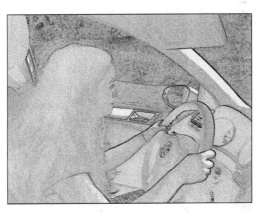

The first time I took you driving after you got your learner's permit – you'll remember we took the winding road that encircles our local park on a quiet weekday afternoon – I told you that you have to be selective, that you have to keep your eye on everything around you and at the same time you should ignore everything except the immediate task at hand.

When you first get behind the wheel, you must train yourself to be aware of all the distractions: The dogs and cats and squirrels that may dart out in front of you, the bicyclists that may not hear you because they're obliviously listening to music bombarding their eardrums as they ride alongside you, the pedestrians who may (or may not) want to cross the street at the upcoming corner. There's a lot that dazzles the senses.

At the same time, you have to shut out all that movement around you, all those diversions and disturbances, and just focus your attention on the mechanics of driving.

Until the feeling of driving comes naturally, you must disregard the driver behind you, who you think may be too aggressive ("I wish he wouldn't get so close!" you said), and the cars that are heading toward you on the other side of the street ("Am I giving them enough room?" you kept asking me), and the elderly couple up ahead, who look like they may want to cross in front of you ("Are they going to cross? Are they?" you wondered).

If you pay too much attention to all that other stuff swirling around, you can lose your focus – after all, you're operating a vehicle that could cause a serious accident, with dire consequences. When you're beginning, you just have to drive within your own abilities, and trust that the rest of the world will take care of itself.

I keep thinking of Emily Dickinson whenever I remember your first driving lessons. "Tell all the truth but tell it slant | Success in circuit lies" she says. She talks about how the truth must "dazzle gradually" or it will blind us. There are some things that must be learned gradually, that must be absorbed over time. We simply can't process too much information taken in too quickly.

You often wonder about the big questions in the world around you. Over the years you have wondered about things that I was not comfortable explaining to you fully at the time, such as questions about why some of our family members are the way they are, about sex and relationships and why marriages sometimes do not work out, about mistakes that I have made over the years.

These days, there is nothing that I keep from you. When you ask me questions I answer the best I can, because I believe that you are now able to absorb and cope with whatever answers, information, and context I can offer.

Learning to drive may not be the most challenging of all activities, but it still takes time to master. Likewise with answers to some of the big questions. Sometimes it is best to pay attention only to what you have to at that moment, and leave the rest for another time. When you were younger I thought it best to provide answers that were appropriate at that time, however incomplete they may have been, and leave the rest of the picture for another time.

Now I trust you are able to take in and understand many more facets of the complete picture, and consider the most inclusive explanations I am able to offer. That is certainly a sign of your maturity, and perhaps of mine as well.

Learn How to Fight

I don't mean that you should learn how to be nasty or cruel. Rather, that you should learn how to disagree with someone – with your own righteous or well-placed anger – and come out on the other side not simmering in dismissiveness or disgust with the opposition you faced.

It doesn't add much to parse this advice too much. I'm not saying that you should "learn to fight." The emphasis is on the "how," on the system and mechanics, so that you're able to separate what you're fighting about from what leads into and results from the fight.

And I am not saying that you should never fight. There will be times that you have to stand your ground, when not to fight is the weakest response you can have, especially when the contrary position may be based on ignorance or prejudice.

The Pakistani activist Malala Yousafzai is an inspiring example of what is possible, even when confronted by crimes against basic freedoms. In her words to the UN defending education for girls she said: "The terrorists thought they would change my aims and stop my ambitions, but nothing changed in my life except this: weakness, fear and hopelessness died. Strength, power and courage was born ... I am not against anyone, neither am I here to speak in terms of personal revenge against the Taliban or any other terrorist group. I'm here to speak up for the right of education for every child."

When you were younger you may remember that I bought a pair of boxing gloves and we used to have boxing matches in the yard. We also made swords – rolled newspaper and lots of duct tape –

A detail from *Jacob Wrestles with the Angel*, by Gustave Doré

and we had fun, and sometimes painful, sword fights. I thought I needed to toughen you up a bit, and these tools seemed appropriate at the time.

Sometimes the most injurious fights are the ones we have with ourselves. One of my brothers, who you never met, was unfortunately a prime example of this. He had, from his childhood, some deep-seated angers. Not public angers – he was very good at presenting a jovial face to the outside world – but they were there, inside. He joined the army and was in Vietnam for about a year. Later he struggled with a series of depressions. His primary adversary, for many years, was himself, and he did not survive those internal fights.

I remember the letters he used to write me from Vietnam (he used to call me "Slick"). Each of the letters, I now realize, hid some foundational self-anger, some bedrock dissatisfaction with his place in the world. As a soldier he fought against others, but he was not able to deal with his own inner demons.

Now that you are out on your own, you will have arguments with others that you do not – perhaps that you cannot or should not – agree with. I hope you have arguments, for example, about the strengths and weaknesses of modernist architecture, about what and how we learn from history, about whether Bach or Mozart is superior.

You may also have arguments about intractable poverty, the place of religion, the role of assisted suicide, and whether prisons offer benefits to society.

You may also have internal struggles, some of which may seem intransigent or impossible at the time. These can be, if you let them, the most difficult.

Having these sorts of struggles are, for better or worse, a very common human trait. They can sharpen the mind, although they can also deaden the senses. Whatever you do, try to make these various situations productive. Try to focus on the "why" and the "how" – without letting the destructive elements define the larger picture.

Failure and Regret and Bravery

Most people, parents and children included, wander through a landscape of regret and failure.

Each of us has ambitions and dreams that we have not fully achieved, desires that we have not realized, hopes that will never come to fruition, and challenges that we think are insurmountable.

Sometimes these feelings of inadequacy are focused on small and inconsequential acts – a task we did that was not rewarded or appreciated as we thought it might be, or an application we made for some job or some award that was disregarded or rejected.

Stewing over these failures and inadequacies can consume large chunks of our spirit and our energy.

From time to time you may even meet people who surprisingly do not know the meaning of regret and failure. It may be safe for these people not to have big dreams or lofty hopes. That way, the effects of the inevitable disappointments are minimized, and easy success can be easily achieved. Some live lives that are small and comfortable and unchallenged. They never feel the invigorating tumult of regret and inadequacy – those forces that can help us strengthen our minds and our sinews to overcome difficulties we may at first think are too big for us.

The trick (yet another trick that we have to play with ourselves) is not to let the disappointment and the fear incapacitate us. Seeking out a droplet of the positive in what can often seem like an ocean of the negative – hanging on to a moment of inner strength within what can seem an all-consuming obstacle or trial – can be a powerful, motivating focus of energy in our lives.

Apsley Cherry-Garrard is one of the all-time great explorers. In the early 1900s he accompanied Robert Falcon Scott's ill-fated attempt to be the first to reach the South Pole.

Cherry-Garrard wrote a book based on that horrific experience called *The Worst Journey in the World*. The book is both chilling and inspiring as he articulates the core of that internal strength needed when confronting incredibly harsh external realities.

On one of his expeditions, he and two others went in search of an un-hatched Emperor Penguin egg in order to do research on penguin feathers, which no one had ever done before. The tale of that journey is breathtaking, in every sense of that word. During one blizzard, with the temperature well below -40, the fierce winds blew the explorers' tent away. Cherry-Garrard shattered most of his teeth shivering and shaking in the severe weather. The cold was so extreme that the liquid in his blisters froze!

Toward the end of his book, Cherry-Garrard talks about the strength it takes to be an explorer (it's important to know that he was so shortsighted that he could barely see without his eyeglasses, which he could not wear hauling his sledge by hand across the frozen Antarctic landscape). If you are brave "you will do nothing," he says, but "if you are fearful you may do much, for none but cowards have need to prove their bravery."

Very few of us get the opportunity to do what Cherry-Garrard did, but all of us benefit from showing personal bravery in the midst of our own inevitable regrets and failures.

Apsley Cherry-Garrard – in my opinion, one of the bravest people who ever lived, even though he used mitten strings. Photograph by Herbert Ponting.

Remembrance of Things Past

I don't remember my father. He died when I was not yet two years old. I only have a few images of him, including a family photograph taken in May 1959. My mother is on one side of the photograph holding my younger sister, and my father is on the other side of the photograph, holding me, the second youngest. My eight other brothers and sisters are arranged haphazardly, fixed in black and white by the photographer. It is a bright day, and all of us are smiling or squinting into the sun, dressed in our best clothes. My father was dead less than two months later.

There is a large part of my familial memory that is non-existent, or that never had the chance to form. It got filled in – as memories do – by other people and other events.

When we are young children, we don't have the ability to remember. Our brains take a while to make the neurological and metaphorical connections. The world comes into shape out of this formless void, as the Bible says, or this shapeless, unwrought chaos, as Ovid calls it.

Or perhaps that's not the way it happens at all. Poet Michael Ondaatje talks about a rich, collective memory that is part of our early lives: "For his first forty days a child / is given dreams of previous lives. / Journeys, winding paths, / a hundred small lessons / and then the past is erased."

Memories, and how we hold on to them, are selective, and idiosyncratic, and sometimes beyond our control. Your maternal grandmother is now suffering from Alzheimer's disease, and although the kindness and gentleness that has always defined her is still very much present, she cannot remember who you are or who her daughter – your mother – is. For her, and my ability to recall my father, and the child in Ondaatje's poem, the past is erased.

It is up to each of us to remember portions of the world. Together, these disparate strands of memory, these diaphanous wisps of the tactile and the tangible, help create a more complete picture of what it means to be alive,

A plasticine picture you made, at age nine, for Father's Day: You and me climbing trees together at our local park.

of our personal and collective history, and perhaps also what we will need to sustain us in the future.

Now that you are out on your own you will be building new memories – gathering moments and traditions out of the air, and preserving them for yourself and (when you share them in stories and conversations) for the rest of us.

Some of these memories will reshape and recast you, so that the more you think about the past, the more your future will shift and adapt. Some will slip away, quickly or slowly, or will be folded into other memories. But it is important to remember that you have the capacity for holding a multitude of memories, and together they'll help shape the person you are and the person you become.

I hope that my ethereal memories of my father live on, in some fashion, through you, however intangible their foundation.

Voices, Voices Everywhere

All of us hear voices.

I don't mean the voice of God or the gods speaking to us through divine revelation, or through religious conversions that occur on the pathways we travel every day. Nor do I mean reveling in the handiwork of some delicate power seen in the elegance of a butterfly's wing or a snow-embroidered mountaintop.

I mean those internal voices that take up such a large part of our interior landscape.

When we are kids we constantly listen to and talk with these voices, whether they are made-up people, animals or things ... or whether they are elements of ourselves. You used to do this, as all kids do, so it must be both inevitable and healthy.

As we get older these voices can be contradictory, repetitious, self-defeating, ecstatic, silly, or just meddlesome. But they are there. They continue on their rambunctious way without us really having the ability to quiet or soften them.

Navigating through them is hard work. Trying to figure out whether we should follow their circuitous logic, or how to lessen the tumultuous noise that they sometimes make has driven some people to depression or madness.

Sometimes people are convinced that the voices come from a higher power. In George Bernard Shaw's play, *Saint Joan*, about the teenaged mystic warrior Joan of Arc, Joan is trying to convince Captain Robert de Baudricourt of the source of her convictions. She says to Robert: "I hear voices telling me what to do. They come from God." Robert responds, a little testily: "They come from your imagination." Joan, always a force of divine inspiration, replies, with all the naïveté of the true believer: "Of course. That is how the messages of God come to us."

In the actual trial record of Joan, which dates from the 1420s, she says she is willing to stop wearing men's clothes (a major crime back then, it seems) but she does "not deny or intend to deny" her "apparitions," or that she hears "voices."

Joan's words, spoken out of fundamental faith – in God, in her own ability to hear God, in her fearless acceptance of the message – are impossible to argue with. Her words may be groundless and her resulting actions may border on the obsessive or the crazed, but that really doesn't matter.

What does matter is that she believes them. Joan puts into action her internal voices, and it's not that dissimilar from others at the ill-defined edges of society who also follow voices: Children, artists, scientists, explorers, entrepreneurs.

These internal forces are not always healthy, and the results of listening to them is not always positive. But they can give us energy and a sense of purpose. The trick is to have some sense of context and some sense of realism. But not too much, because that only quiets the voices, which in turn quiets the imagination. As with most interesting things in our lives, there are no easy answers.

I encourage you to listen to the voices – after all, you don't really have a choice. Act on them as you see fit, realizing that they may not always lead to sensible or logical ends.

Whatever you do, don't ignore the voices. Shutting them out, or pretending they are not there, lessens your sympathy for others, and belittles your own sense of creativity and imagination.

Joan of Arc, in an anonymous painting from around 1485. The artist has given us three separate voices speaking to Joan.

A Multitude of Truths

Woven into many of our conversations over the years – as we comment on TV, radio, and podcasts; as we talk about your friends or teachers; as we tell stories about family members – I've always tried to impress upon you how strongly I believe that there are a multitude of stories and truths that make up the world. There is not just one true story. Not only one path toward truth. Not one singular religion that holds all the answers.

Even when you have been definitive in your opinions – about capital punishment or assisted suicide or other contentious topics that you have studied and sometimes written papers on in school – I try to toss at you variant opinions and other ways of interpreting the information you have in front of you.

"Yes, but there are other ways to see the same information," I may say. Or "Well, if what you say is true, then this also must be true … which doesn't really make sense, does it?"

I've tried not to be too dogmatic with you, but the one thing I am dogmatic about is that there is not one dogma that is necessarily and absolutely better than the others.

As you meet more and more people from larger and larger circles, some may try to convince you that their religion and their holy book is more right than the others. They may tell you, for example, that the Bible should be taken literally. That it is the word of God and should be followed and believed in, verbatim.

Like many great books, the Bible is full of metaphor, of conflicting interpretations, of stories that try to explain things for which we may never have an explanation. But it is not a work of inviolable truth, nor is it meant to be.

The book of Genesis itself is internally inconsistent. It has two distinct stories of creation. In Genesis 1:27 we are told that on the sixth day God created man and woman "So God created man in his *own* image, in the image of God created he him; male and female created he them." And then in Genesis 2:7, we are told that it was not until the seventh day that God created people, and then only man first: "And the Lord God formed man of the dust of the ground, and breathed into his nostrils the breath of life; and man became a living soul." In this second version of the creation, women do not appear until Genesis 2:21-22: "And the Lord God caused a deep sleep to fall upon Adam, and he slept; and he took one of his ribs, and closed up the flesh instead thereof; And the rib, which the Lord God had taken from man, made he a woman, and brought her unto the man."

Both of these versions of creation cannot simultaneously be true. Either God created man and woman at the same time, or man first. Either God created man and woman on the sixth day, or the seventh day.

Should people you meet try to convince you that the Bible is to be followed as though it were truth or fact, and not a work of metaphor or story, remind them that there are indeed multiple ways to see the world, multiple possible explanations for our central mysteries, and the Bible is living proof of that.

There are many ways to see and describe the world. Here are the beginnings of various alphabets, from an early guidebook used by engravers. The languages are (left to right) Cuneiform, Runic, Arabic, Armenian, Hebrew, Japanese, and Tibetan.

33

Be Strong

There are, of course, many ways to be strong. One can be strong physically, intellectually, emotionally, spiritually, psychologically, etc.

As for physical strength, you may have heard about the "World's Strongest Man" competition, where men of some bulk test their strength in various events, including the Hercules Hold (contestants stand between hinged pillars, tying to prevent them from falling to the side), the Keg Toss (kegs of increasing weight are thrown over a high steel wall), and Atlas Stones (round stones weighing up to about 350 pounds are carried and assembled on top of high platforms).

But you may not have heard of, or even know how to pronounce the name of *Archegozetes longisetosus*. These teeny-tiny mites – they measure about 1/32 of an inch – have been called the strongest living things on earth. Measuring the strength of these little dynamos, scientists determined that they have a pull-force equal to 1,150 times their own weight. Putting this in human terms, it would be like a 150-pound person lifting an 86-ton whale. In animal terms, it would be like an elephant carrying a tower of 1,150 elephants on its back.

Here are a few more facts about these remarkable creatures. All of the individuals are female. They have been reproducing by parthenogenesis (a form of asexual reproduction where life begins without fertilization) for a very long time.

Scientists like studying them because they have a short lifespan, and because they are relatively easily cultured in a laboratory. Individuals lay eggs every few days.

One of these mighty mites carrying Atlas on her back, who carries the world on his back.

There are small beetles that often live in the same area that the mites do and the beetles like to feed on them. But the mites have developed a chemical defense against being eaten: They have oil glands on their bodies that the beetles do not like. However, the main reason that scientists have given them so much attention is because of their incredible strength.

You too have great strength within you, including your ability to ask tough questions, sometimes so clearly and so insightfully that it leaves me in awe, almost breathless. "Why did she die?" you asked, when you were told that your music teacher had been killed while on her first tour to promote her first album release. "Why don't people accept other people – especially those who are different from them?" you once asked in a moment of pure and inspired anger.

You don't always realize the power and effect of your own inner strengths: Your ability to celebrate the achievements and success of your friends, and your ability to recognize when a friend needs help about some personal trouble they're having, and how you might be able to support them.

Anne Frank is a symbol of strength in the midst of horrific circumstances. At the age of 15 she wrote in her diary: "It's difficult in times like these: ideals, dreams and cherished hopes rise within us, only to be crushed by grim reality. It's a wonder I haven't abandoned all my ideals ... Yet I cling to them because I still believe, in spite of everything, that people are truly good at heart." There is profound and courageous strength within her teenage words.

Continue to be strong and to nourish your strengths. And learn about different types of strength whenever you can, and from whatever source. Remember that you don't have to be big to be strong. Very small beings, and very small acts, can have great strength.

Judge for Yourself

Who knows all of the things you're going to try in the coming few years? And who knows the motivations and impulses behind these various decisions?

You may help tutor children who have had many less advantages than you've had. You may work at the school newspaper, interviewing and talking with people you sharply disagree with. You may start a new band, or take a year off, or decide to study subjects just because of some passing fancy, or spend a chunk of your time helping one of your co-workers who is struggling through some sort of personal trauma. You may volunteer in a soup kitchen or with young entrepreneurs.

Whatever you do, don't let yourself be defined or judged by others. Don't allow others to measure your life, restrict your imaginings, or limit your desires.

Some people, however well intentioned, may try to convince you to follow their script, may try to bend you toward their own way of addressing or confronting the world. Some will pigeonhole you because of the money you have or because of the money you don't have. Still others may label you too much of a victim, or too privileged to know any better, or too hard, or too soft.

Woven in and throughout the many decisions that you'll be making, and surrounded by friends both new and old doing the same thing, you will inevitably make mistakes. We all do. You may make the same mistake a few times – that also is not such an unusual thing. Often the biggest mistakes we make teach us the most.

Although we all consider and evaluate others – weighing ourselves against others, and others against ourselves – don't allow yourself to define and judge others too much. They also are going though similar, or different, questions on whatever road they've chosen. They too have their own pockets of ignorance and their own blind spots. They have their own motivations.

George Eliot, one of the greatest of all novelists, and whom you will likely read in the years ahead, is a good person to consider when thinking about judging others. Not considered physically attractive, and therefore not a likely candidate for marriage, her father instead invested in her education. She lived for over 20 years with George Henry Lewes, who because of Victorian standards could not divorce his wife. Born Mary Ann Evans, she wrote under the pen name George Eliot to ensure that her works were taken seriously, and to avoid the stereotypes that others

Four images of Mary Ann Evans, also known as George Eliot, which range from the representational to the idealized.

had of female writers. After Lewes died, she again bucked tradition, this time by marrying a man 20 years her junior. Throughout these various twists and turns she wrote seven novels, including *Middlemarch*, which some consider the greatest novel in the English language (an assessment I'm tempted to agree with).

In *Middlemarch*, George Eliot talks about how we don't always follow a straight, well-defined path to get where we're going: "starting a long way off the true point, and proceeding by loops and zig-zags, we now and then arrive just where we ought to be."

It was also George Eliot who said, in *The Mill on the Floss*, "Don't judge a book by its cover." Wise words, those.

Green and Dying

I remember driving with you and your friend Lauren one day – it may have been after one of your singing/dancing/acting classes that you took every summer for a few years. Lauren had been reading the poem "Do Not Go Gentle Into That Good Night" by Dylan Thomas and she was pleased with herself for being able to recite a few lines from the poem. I too was happy to hear those words coming from the back seat. It was fun to hear a 14-year-old talking about raging at the dying of the light.

Occupied with their own sense of eternal discovery, children don't often consider the ravages of time and age, but Thomas certainly did, and you will perhaps consider these things more and more as you get older.

In another of Thomas's poems, "Fern Hill," he talks within those musical lines about seeing things as they pass, and about how it is time – we are in the "mercy of his means" says Thomas – that allows us to hail and climb and play and be.

"Time held me green and dying," says Thomas. The poem has this marvelous ability to capture both the excitements of youth and the gathering, relentless end that we all move toward.

You have already experienced a fair share of dying (your maternal grandfather, your music and voice teacher, and others), and you've experienced a fair share of birth (your cousins, the children you used to babysit, and others). Perhaps if we totaled them up, there would be equal numbers of deaths and births.

Is age and the approach of death more noticeable in and through me (in my late-fifties) or in and through you (in your late teens)? Probably in and through me, although I'm not really sure.

Both of us are aging at the same rate, even if our spirits and minds and bodies are not the same age. In a vacuum, says Galileo, things of different weight fall at the same rate. Perhaps the same is true of people. Although I am forty years older than you, we are still aging (still falling) at exactly the same rate through this vacuum of time.

Both of us are simultaneously green (enthusiastic, full of questions, at times anxious) and dying (aging, filling up with memories, at times fearful) and perhaps the best we can do is sustain that tension for as long as we can.

Beauty is Skin-Deep and Soul-Deep

Much of our society is in the business of physical beauty. Obsessions about this most fleeting and facile aspect sometimes take up the most attention. The make-up industry, the diet industry, the plastic surgery industry, the health club industry, as well as the soap and fragrance and skin-care industries: They all feed off our self-indulgence and insecurity, and all consume huge parts of our resources. (You may be interested to know that in the U.S. more is spent each year on beauty than on education.)

But perhaps we can draw comfort of sorts when we realize that humans have always been concerned with these skin-deep fixations. Juvenal, the ancient Roman poet, satirizes women who slather on so much make-up, scents, and lotions that once their work is done it's unclear what's underneath all that, a "face or an ulcer"!

Medieval women dabbed the blood of bats on their faces to spruce up their complexions; women in 18th-century America used the warm urine of young boys to help erase freckles; and Victorian women sometimes had their own ribs removed so that their waists were thinner and therefore presumably more attractive to their Victorian husbands and lovers.

As a young woman you have already been inflicted with all sorts of advertising ploys related to so-called beauty. I often feared that they were seeping into your otherwise healthy sense of self-worth without you truly realizing it.

Over the years, starting with our very first conversations, I have said to you many times (hundreds? thousands?): "You are the smartest and most beautiful girl in the whole wide world." I've said it to you so many times because I wanted you to absorb the words with the same ease

that you drink water or feel the breeze on your skin. And I always wanted to connect the idea of being "smart" with the idea of being "beautiful" (and in that order). I've always thought that these two qualities were inextricable.

I still happen to believe this about you, and I still tell you this, although not as frequently as when you were younger. My fear now is that you think I'm just being patronizing or kindly when I say it, but that's okay. I will likely continue using this phrase – or some version of it – until our final conversations.

Mathematicians talk about the beauty of numbers, astronomers talk about the beauty of interstellar space, and geneticists talk about the beauty found within our gene sequences. Many visual artists do not, curiously, talk about beauty, because these days it is seen to be a rather quaint and old-fashioned way to explain and articulate what artists do.

The Renaissance priest and scientist Nicolas Steno differentiated among various depths of beauty, from the tangible to the intangible. He said: "Beautiful are the things we see, more beautiful are those we understand, the most beautiful are those we do not comprehend."

I hope you never lose sight of the different types of beauty that exist, and of the different ways that beauty can be appreciated. And please do remember that I think you are the smartest and most beautiful young woman in the whole wide world.

The Wonderful in the Common

 There is always the wonderful within the common, the mysterious hidden within the mundane. I always remember the small moments of wonder and beauty and love that we've shared over the years.

As a small child, you would sometimes point to a bit of rainbow, refracted through an edge of beveled glass, as it comes to life on the wall. The colors live and shift form for a few moments – spilling their charms into our lives – and then they slip away.

Or one of us would point out a patch of tree bark that had a particularly beautiful texture – it looked like the waves of the sea, or sand dunes rippling across the desert – and then we would continue on our walk or our errand.

Or we'd see a bug lazily sunning itself on the sidewalk – a crispy, blue-black body glistening in the sunlight – and then we'd say "Hi!" to one of your friends who happened to be passing by, or we'd cross the street and head off for an ice cream cone.

Sometimes we would never even exchange words. One of us would just point at the fleck of wonder before us, we'd both look intently for a few seconds, and then we'd be off. The yellow-throated bird, or the scrap of cloud that looked remarkably like a frog, may not have been there a moment before and would not be there a moment later – we just happened to have caught it at the perfect time.

Once while walking among the bookstalls in London, during my third year of university spent in Europe, I came upon a very curious book, published in 1720. I bought it for a few pounds (it was moldy and in pretty rough shape). It still brings me moments of rare pleasure. It's called *A Discourse of the Several Dignities, and Corruptions, of Man's Nature, since the Fall,* and it's written by "the Ever Memorable Mr. John Hales of Eton." I'm not sure anyone still remembers the "Ever Memorable" Mr. John Hales, but he does have some endearing things to say in the midst of his turgid tract.

"It is itself prejudicial to the Advancement of Knowledge, to pass by all ordinary Occurrences without any Notice, or Admiration, and to think nothing wonderful that is common," he says.

You have certainly helped me see many wonderful things among the common. All children do, to parents who are attentive. Children are delighted by new things, and everything is new to them. They are intrigued by everything they learn, and the world is full of things that they are learning for the first time. They like things that are different, and to them everything is different.

Your questions and observations – about people and butterflies and trees and music – have always amazed me with their sense of astonishment and acceptance and affection.

Children see beauty everywhere. You love the things that are around you because that is the most natural way to understand the world. It is the most intuitive way for all children, including you, to connect with the world that you see, smell, taste, touch, and hear.

It's important for adults, for fathers, to remember these fleeting moments of beauty and how they are so naturally a part of how children absorb the world around them.

Focus!

There are two ways to focus your attention: Use a microscope or use a telescope.

When I was a kid and had some question or concern for my mom – including such items of monumental importance as "Why can't I borrow the car?" or "Why do I have to cut the grass right now!" or "Tell Patty [my sister] to stop bugging me!" – she would simple say to me, in a calming voice: "Don't worry about it, dear. What difference will it make ten years from now?"

And when I could not find some specific thing I had been looking for – a misplaced baseball mitt, the key for my bike lock, my school book-bag – she would say to me, with motherly insight: "Look with your eyes, and you'll find what you're looking for."

I'm not sure at the time that I really absorbed either type of wisdom my mom offered me – confronted by what could be considered a big issue, consider the long view and the current struggle won't seem so daunting after all; confronted by a small task, narrow the view and concentrate on the immediate task at hand. I guess I did eventually come to understand the idea of perspective and focus my mom was helping me uncover. Or at least I've come to some understanding now, and that's why I pass on to you these focusing wisdoms that my mother inspired in me.

These wisdoms can certainly be adapted to your new life. When things get a bit harried – perhaps you have three papers due in the same week, or you're having trouble juggling your work schedule and the different assignments you are responsible for – it can help to take a step back. At these times it's beneficial to appreciate the long view, trusting

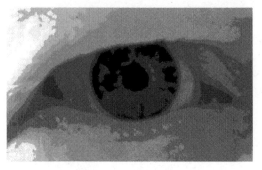 that things over the long run will sort themselves out, that the tumult of conflicting tasks will quiet down, and that you will eventually find your own rhythm through or around the conflicts. You're sure to find your way forward,

and what difference will these testy challenges really have ten years from now anyway?

And when the smaller arcs of your life appear to lack continuity and logic, when it seems like the trivial tasks are piling up and threatening to overwhelm you, it can help to narrow your focus to the immediate job at hand, trusting that well-defined, sequential activities eventually lead to some sense of greater equilibrium and coherence.

The talent, of course, comes in figuring out which focus is best suited to the immediate circumstances – whether to pinpoint your attentions (concentrating on the small, illustrative details) or to widen your attentions (concentrating on the expanse and inclusiveness of the larger picture).

Being human, we're not always very good at deciding which is the best point of focus. I know I certainly am not. But sometimes (perhaps because it can be easier to see in another what we cannot see in ourselves) we can help others when they seem to be floundering with similar questions.

Remember that you have always been able to find your direction and your path, even if the beginning of the way can seem mislabeled or hidden by a forest of conflicting pressures. Perhaps it all comes down to trusting in yourself. Trust that you will eventually find the relevant path forward, whether it be large or small. That self-trust is a good thing to focus on.

I Am, Therefore I Think

We have art and religion and science because we have the ability to imagine art and religion and science. We also have war and evil and ignorance because we have the ability to imagine war and evil and ignorance. We cannot help ourselves. Being human means that our minds — the synapses carrying chemical and electrical signals (and the attendant ideas and symbols) — are always at work.

"I think, therefore I am," says Descartes. But it is just as true to say: "I am, therefore I think."

Now that you are heading out on your own — expanding your circle of friends, contacts, and acquaintances, and meeting new people from vastly divergent backgrounds — you'll be talking with many people who think differently from you. Not necessarily better or worse — but differently.

From an early cover page of *Meditations on First Philosophy* by Rene Descartes.

Some of the people you meet will, I hope, dazzle you with the energetic enthusiasm of their insights and ideas. Some will likely have opinions that you question or with which you violently disagree.

I've had many conversations with people who have superstitions, conspiracy theories, and beliefs that have me shaking my head and wondering how they could possibly come to believe what they do.

You are now truly learning to navigate your own path and at your own pace – learning to avoid branches that can knock you on your butt, or stepping back from the slippery edge of a cliff that overlooks the sharp rocks far below. The same talents for navigating people also apply. The swirling ideas that will confront you – from every single person you meet and from the tumultuous accumulation of all these ideas – will often have you scratching your head or wondering how people could possibly come to think the way they do.

Sometimes their ideas will be presented with conviction, statistics, and evidence that can be quite compelling. But don't be fooled by misguided conviction, faulty statistics, or flimsy evidence. Just because we all think – in fact, thought comes so naturally to us that we can't help it, stop it, or even tamp it down – doesn't mean that we all think with the same sense of objectivity, insight, and wonder that Descartes had.

Our thoughts, always on the move, can stray far afield without a clear direction and without strong foundations. Sometimes they swim into dead-end caves of ignorance or misplaced belief. Sometimes they fly into the full force of hurricanes and tornadoes, swirling with debris and anger.

Relish this tumult of divergent thinking. Enjoy the discussions, arguments, and debates you'll be a part of. Weigh and ponder how and why you come to your own conclusions.

But also be wary – and dubious – of some of the things you'll be confronted with. You have developed instincts about what to believe and to act on, and what to avoid or to question. Now you'll really get the chance to test those instincts.

It Ain't That Serious

You have said a lot of funny things in your life. All children do, especially when they are learning to speak. They constantly mix things up, or can't find the right words for the things they're trying to express.

As you got older you started to show a more constructed form of humor – an outlet, perhaps, for your desire to entertain and amuse.

When you were six years old you wrote and illustrated a small book called "Duckie's Snow Day" (complete with apostrophe, I'm happy to say). The book was a way for you to talk about, I imagine, the trials and tribulations of getting ready to go outside on a cold, wintery day. Here is the text of these 11 pages, and a description of each accompanying illustration:

- This is the Duckie's owner. *(A sleeping girl is pictured beneath a window, with huge snowflakes descending.)*
- One nice winter morning Duckie looked out .... *(A cut-out duck is taped on to the page, beneath the snowy window.)*
- ... His window and for a surprise he saw snow. *(A hand-drawn duck this time, and the window again.)*
- This is Duckie's friend. *(A little dog among purple flowers looks out at the reader.)*
- I am going outside, said Duckie. *(A hand-drawn duck awaits the adventures outdoors.)*
- Where's my hat? said Duckie. Here it is. *(Duckie is now wearing a red hat.)*

- ○ Where is my coat? Here it is. *(Duckie is now wearing the hat and a coat.)*
- ○ Where is my scarf? Here it is. *(Duckie is now wearing the hat, coat and scarf.)*
- ○ Where are my earmuffs? Here they are. *(Duckie is now wearing the red hat, red coat, red scarf, and red earmuffs.)*
- ○ Where is the snow? *(Similar Duckie to previous illustration, still all dressed and ready to go.)*
- ○ It melted! *(No illustration.)*

Of course, I appreciate the power of the progressive questions that Duckie asks, the ascending rhetorical and graphic skill of dressing the Duckie, the theoretical awareness of the audience, and the ironic flick ending, certainly worthy of those world-renowned writers of short stories, O. Henry or Guy de Maupassant.

You have also shown other sorts of humor. When you were 10 you gave me a book of "PUNISHMENT COUPONS" which were meant, I guess, to provide a counterpoint to more pleasant sorts of rewards. They included: "This coupon good for giving ME a foot massage" and "This coupon good for NOT giving me a kiss" and "This coupon good for me doing the dishes for money."

When you were 14 and started to wear make-up, I once asked you why, being so cute, you chose to wear make-up. Your response: "Dad, I wear make-up to hide the pimples that the make-up causes!"

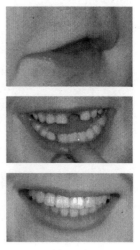

Recently you and I came upon a book, *Getting Pregnant*, which someone had left at the entrance to our apartment building, at the spot where items are placed when people want to get rid of them. "Hey, that's my book!" you said, as we passed by.

I hope you continue on these funny ways.

Some of your smiles – from 7 days old, and 7 years old, and 17 years old.

All Opinion is Local

Of one thing I am sure: Throughout your self-supporting, independent life you will be confronted, buffeted, and whiplashed by a wide and disparate assortment of opinions and viewpoints. In fact, I hope you are, because confronting all this noise is the best way to determine what you believe and think.

These opinions and viewpoints are not always based on hard data, or well thought out, or even sensible. But as you'll discover, a strongly articulated opinion does not always need to be logical in order to sway allegiances and gather followers.

A detail from "Credulity, Superstition and Fanaticism," by William Hogarth. The artist knew a few things about "excessive enthusiasm" and how such opinions influence our religious, secular, political, and economic life.

History is filled with passionately held opinions that have hung on for years or centuries – or even longer – with no logic or sense behind them.

Sometimes the opinions have great wisdom at their core. Plato's dialogues about ideas and forms have been with us for about 2,500 years and they are still parsed and explored to this day. Aristotle, a student of Plato's, wrote foundational texts on literature and literary theory.

Sometimes the opinions have great ignorance at their core, or at least from the vantage point of our era. There have been otherwise intelligent people who believed that women should not vote, that slavery was defensible, and that the earth was the center of the universe.

Many lives have been lost and much blood spilt on such fanatical debates as to how many angels can dance on the head of a pin, on how to prevent so-called witches from driving us to the devil, and on whether global warming is a myth or reality.

I sometimes wonder what people will think centuries or millennia from now about our current era. Will they look back and wonder why we filled our air with toxins, why it took us so long to discover and encourage essential freedoms, and how we could have encouraged and enabled endless wars between countries and religions and cultures?

Or perhaps they will not have the time or inclination to look back on the wayward delusions of past ages because they will be so preoccupied with their own wayward delusions.

Throughout this eternal windstorm of conflicting and sometimes despicable opinions, you really have to resort to your own inner strength, your own sense of healthy skepticism, your own set of beliefs that you have been developing since you were a child.

Many human beings never spend time seeking or finding sensible and coherent answers. Some are very good at asking questions. Perhaps that is the best place to start. And maybe even the best place to end.

Sex

This may be the one topic that young women such as you believe their parents have nothing – absolutely nothing – of any value to add.

You may say: "How is it possible that parents can even vaguely understand what I'm going through and what my desires and needs are?"

Or: "You are from the ancient times – 40 years ago – and things have changed drastically since then. Any opinions you may have are hopelessly outdated."

Or simply: "Sorry. Too much information. Next subject please!"

Perhaps these are inevitable and healthy ways of saying that you want and need to learn about this stuff for yourself. But there are some basics, which all parents, you may be interested to know, have also gone through.

We're all here because of sex. It's that simple. If people thousands of years ago and hundreds of years ago and decades ago did not have sex, none of us would be here.

But perhaps there is more to say on the topic.

Sex can be the most enjoyable, fraught, disturbing, and essential activity there is. Sometimes all simultaneously. It's not the same thing as love, but they can be connected. And boys and girls, men and women, often think differently about sex and love.

Perhaps because sex is so central to our lives, human beings have developed all sorts of rules and regulations, all sorts of beliefs and theories, about it. Many of these have changed over time, even if at one point they were connected to rigid societal laws, seemingly eternal religions, and other such overarching organizing principles.

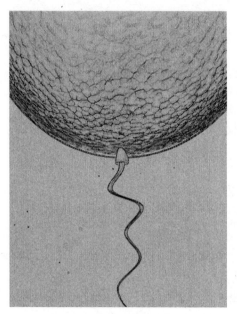

But sex, somehow, always triumphs. No amount of ruling or regulating has stopped the centrality of sex, the inevitability of sex. The joys of sex.

And, really, is there much to talk about, especially when it is the most natural activity there is? My mom had 10 children and then brought up another 12 stepchildren – so she knew a few things.

There is always lots to learn about the central mystery of our very human natures.

Yet she and I never spoke about sex. I guess she thought that one way or another, I'd figure things out for myself. And she was right, of course, about this as she was about so many other things.

Perhaps the only real knowledge I can pass on is that in the middle of those uncontrollable and anarchic impulses, try as well to be mindful. Try to think about the acts and ideas related to sex that are not purely physical. There are other forms of attraction (I don't say "better" or "higher" forms of attraction) than sex. One of them is love. Another is respect. Another is the human desire to connect with other humans at the most elemental level.

I'm certainly still learning about all this – sex is, after all, one of the great and good mysteries. And I hope you constantly learn too, throughout your life.

Be True to What?

"To thine own self be true," says the paternalistic old windbag Polonius in Shakespeare's play *Hamlet*.

Some readers see a few drops of wisdom in these words, but they follow a checklist of rather insignificant scraps of advice that Polonius has just dispensed: Make sure you keep good company, don't borrow or lend money, listen attentively but don't speak too much, blah, blah, blah.

And really, what does "To thine own self be true" mean anyway?

It's pretty easy to be true to yourself if you decide to have a narrow and restrictive view of the world – if you keep your sights small and your skepticism to a minimum. I've known lots of people who are true to themselves because they have so little to be true to that the task is quite easy. And ultimately that's not a very fulfilling way to live.

My advice to you (and I hope I'm not sounding too Polonian here) is: Don't decide to be true to yourself

An early engraving of Polonius, finger-wagging and giving his rather simplistic advice.

until you've done some wondering, some wandering, some struggling, and some questioning.

We all need context and points of comparison. We all need to see viewpoints that we disagree with, to meet people we would not choose to emulate, and to doubt what others sometimes present to us as perfect, good, and worthy.

We all need to discover what others mean by the "true" and the "self." And then we need to discover what we ourselves mean by the "true" and the "self." It's not an easy task and I've always been wary of those who think the path toward self-insight is a straightforward and gentle slope.

How can we possibly be true to our ideas and ideals when we are not sure how and why we are on the road we've chosen; how can we possibly know our self when we haven't experienced multiple perspectives for comparison?

Don't forget that Hamlet refers to Polonius as a "tedious old fool." Although Hamlet may not be the paragon of decisiveness, he does have self-insight and a passion to see that the truth is made evident, even if he never arrives at his own understanding of peaceful truth.

So by all means, be true to yourself, but make sure that you've done some exploring and some questioning before you settle too quickly on your chosen path, or paths. This exploring and questioning quickens the blood. As the poet and teacher Maya Angelou says: "believing that life loves the liver of it, I have dared to try many things, sometimes trembling, but daring, still."

And never let anyone else define for you what the "true" is and what the "self" is. You are smart enough to figure out those things for yourself.

P P & F

I remember as a kid – maybe around the age of nine – asking my mom what the word "infinity" meant.

She said to me: Just imagine a tall mountain, and every hundred years a bird flies over the top of that mountain, and as it flies by its wing just brushes the top of the mountain. When that mountain is worn down as flat as the prairies that will be just the very beginning of infinity.

As a kid I didn't fully absorb the many layers of meaning and time that were wrapped up in that story my mom told me. It was the sort of simple, powerful image that can take a lifetime, or more, to absorb.

My mom died about 20 years ago. I have photographs of her looking youthful and glamorous – as a young girl of about nine among her immediate family of four brothers and five sisters, as a teenager holding a tennis racket and smiling like she was having the time of her life, of her stepping out of an airplane with my dad, both of them just back from some international adventure.

Now as I see you heading out on your own – with a foundational part of your life already over, and heading off to other grand adventures that will last for a few years or a few decades – I realize, once again, how connected the past, present, and future are.

Albert Einstein said that "the distinction between past, present and future is only a stubbornly persistent illusion." Although Einstein meant this in a scientific context – he knew that time is fluid, malleable, relative – in our imaginations too the distinctions between the past, present, and future are illusory.

My mom's story, contained within a few moments of the past that she and I shared, is with me now in the present as I wonder and marvel at your future, spreading out before you like a marvelous colored tapestry that you will be a part of shaping, crafting, and decorating.

There are an infinite variety of ways that we can relive the past, shape the present, and build the future. And perhaps it helps to appreciate that within the eternal present – the infinitesimal instant of our life that we live in, which is simultaneously informed by our past and anticipating our future – there are a world of possibilities.

You have an infinity of time before you – both the protean time that came before you, and the abundant time that is spreading out before you into the future – and I hope that you enjoy and appreciate each of the moments of past, present, and future that make up this infinity.

Connecting the past, present and future – my mom, around the age of nine, with the reflection of a father in the background, who is anticipating and imagining your future.

Words Made Flesh

It has taken me a long time to figure out what to say about tattoos because I know that it really doesn't matter what I say – you will decide of your own free will, and out of your own personal, cultural and societal norms, whether or not you're going to get a tattoo, or multiple tattoos.

The only thing I can say, which may have some sticking power, is to think first before you get a tattoo – not about what it will say or illustrate, but why you're getting it.

I've come to realize it's not really tattoos that I'm unenthusiastic about. It's that they are often facile clichés such as "Carpe Diem" or "UNIQUE" permanently etched onto your skin, or they are poorly drawn images of Elvis Presley or one's grandmother that will surely droop as the tattooed skin gets older and looser, or they are too much concerned with an external gesture of showing off.

I am all for exploring the way each of us fits into, or does not fit into, the orthodoxy of the world's rules and laws. In fact I think this is one of our principal responsibilities – to investigate how we connect to ourselves and to others. The answers, it seems to me, are often found in our own core, not in the adornments we present to the outside world.

The poet W. B. Yeats believes that the "root of reality" is at the "center" of our lives and not in "that whirling circumference" of the outside world.

He also says that we should honor those people who show reckless "courage in entering into the abyss" of themselves.

And here is one of my favorite quotations by Yeats: "Be secret and exult, | Because of all things known | That is most difficult."

These snippets of Yeats speak about the importance of conscientiously and relentlessly exploring the inner life, the life of the imagination and its mystical implications, its intricate responsibilities and its morphing freedoms.

> # Be secret and exult,
>
> # Because of all things known
>
> # That is most difficult.

If I were to get a tattoo, this is the one I'd get. And then I'd keep it hidden so I was the only one who knew it was there.

It can be too easy to trumpet to the outside world what we think we know and what we think we believe. It is more challenging, I believe, to go inside ourselves. Searching for our own internal symbols can be more difficult, but ultimately more rewarding, than seeking and celebrating external symbols.

The recent tattoo fad – I know I'm simplifying here – seems to me more about the external than the internal, more about the flash and sparkle than about insight and self-knowledge.

Of course everyone who has a tattoo is proud of it and wants to show it off. If you decide to make a permanent gesture for the outside world you too would want to make sure that the outside world is well aware of your commitment. How can you regret something that you were so convinced was right at the time, and now may take significant resources and a lot of pain to remove? Better just to go with it, especially if many around you are doing the same.

So get a tattoo or multiple tattoos if you want, but just be mindful that there are other ways of exploring and embellishing yourself. Sometimes the strongest gestures only have an audience of one.

No, You Don't Have to Be Negative

You will hear many forms of the word "no" over your years at college and in your workplaces. People who believe that if you truly think about the world you have to come away pessimistic. Others who are convinced that degradation of various sorts (rapacious financial markets, the collapse of the environment, the rise of religious fundamentalism, the dictatorship of technology) is simply the landscape through which we wander now.

There are others who may be negative to you directly, convinced that you do not have the intellectual context or independence or sensitivity or strength to pursue whatever it is you are attempting.

And then there are the natural, internal thoughts of negativity that we all have. All of us have self-doubts: Insecurities and weaknesses that we try to hide from the world, swaths of illiteracy or inexperience for which we try to compensate, and nagging and sometimes incapacitating lack of confidence. "I've never done that before," we tell ourselves. "I'm no good at this." "I'll never be able to do that."

Despite what humans have always believed, the world is not getting worse, is not disintegrating. Literary critic Northrop Frye highlighted an inscription unearthed after 5,000 years. This ancient text opined:

"Children no longer obey their parents, and the end of the world is rapidly approaching." And 2,500 years ago Socrates said: "Our children now love luxury. They have bad manners, contempt for authority; they show disrespect for their elders and love chatter in place of exercise." And on through to our own age, from Gore Vidal, who wrote a book called *The Decline and Fall of the American Empire* to this morning's print or online newspaper.

Don't believe it.

Of course the world is a fallible place, full of ignorant, insignificant, and inferior things. There will always be "apocaholics" (people who exploit and profit from the natural pessimism of human nature, as geneticist and rational optimist Matt Ridley says). But so too there is the opportunity for infinite progress, continuous work to improve our lot, and potential for you and your friends to make positive, lasting change. The Internet optimistically encourages the cross-fertilization of ideas and the democratization of knowledge – and this is the world in which you find yourself.

When I first went off to college a friend from my high school told me that his father once said to him: Don't be too hard on yourself. The world can be a negative and harsh place, full of people telling you that you won't have success and that you can't do what you want to do. Leave that negativity to the outside world. When you talk to yourself, be positive, be optimistic. The world will beat you up – you don't have to beat yourself up too.

My father, who was an optimistic person (with 10 children, he would have had to be), died when I was still quite young and so I never had this sort of wisdom from him directly. But I did take this advice given to my friend from his father, and tried to internalize it and make use of it. I've come to realize that this wisdom is appropriate both when addressing the negativity of the outside word and the negativity that lurks within each of us.

Don't let the world beat you up. Don't beat yourself up. These are not always the easiest words to live by, but the crystalline strengths found within them are preferable and more productive than words of pessimism and negativity. Or as Charles Sigmund, my favorite teacher from high school, wrote in my Grade 12 yearbook: "Don't let the bastards grind you down."

Jealousy (Good and Bad)

I'm jealous of you. I can't help it.

Here you are heading off with limitless enthusiasm and wonder into a world of new knowledge, ideas, and challenges.

Of course it's not all going to be easy and stress-free or without challenges that sometimes seem insurmountable. It never is.

But you'll be learning about the implications of recent discoveries on the origins of the universe – how within the first trillionth of a trillionth of a trillionth of a second the universe grew from something unimaginably small into the size of a grapefruit. Even to put such an observation into words sounds somewhere between spectacularly incomprehensible and simply beautiful.

And you'll be learning about William Blake and the implications of his wrenching poetry – how it is possible for a poet to appreciate what others do not, and then to write: "To See a World in a Grain of Sand / And a Heaven in a Wild Flower." Even to put such an observation into words sounds somewhere between simply incomprehensible and spectacularly beautiful.

Of course there will be jealousies among your fellow students, co-workers, and others you meet. Colleges and workplaces can be filled with jealousies both petty and large. In this sense, colleges and workplaces are no different from other places that you'll be part of in the years and decades to come: Gatherings of friends and family, and clubs or associations you may belong to.

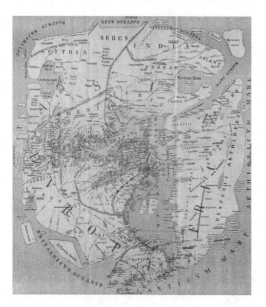

An early map, imagined by Pomponius Mela around 43 CE. How can I not be a bit jealous of you, knowing as I do that the whole world is waiting for you, and you are waiting for the whole world?

Many of us covet what we do not have. Many of us cannot help from swaggering when we have what others do not.

And each of us has insecurities both large and small. Sometimes these insecurities can be fleeting and insignificantly small specks of immaturity that quickly pass – our better natures immediately take over and we find our natural state of equilibrium. At other times these insecurities seem to engulf our whole universe and can consume all of our energies and all of our attentions – our lesser natures stew and worry and over-think, so that we are left with lingering anger or dissatisfaction.

As many have observed: Especially when the jealousies and points of disagreement are small – in fact, because they are so small – the recriminations and implications can be huge and out of all proportion.

But enough about these different types of jealousies. You will surely discover and witness enough of them on your own in the years to follow.

What I really want to say is that at this moment I am jealous of you – and of all the new things that await you. And that perhaps is not such a bad type of jealousy.

Everything is ... Pandemically Speaking ... Relative

As I've mentioned to you a few times (okay, maybe many times), during the great plague of the 1350s, about one-third of the population between India and Iceland died. That is a helluva lot of people.

And during the 60 months of World War II, about 60,000,000 people died. That's an average of 1,000,000 people every month for 60 months.

Why am I bringing up these horrifically dark moments from our collective history? To remind you that people – our civilizations and our cultures – have gone through monstrously terrible times ... and survived.

Historians and artists can help us remember the atrocities that nature or that we ourselves inflict. Often we find ways to flourish after massive tragedies. It is generally acknowledged that the terrible years of the great plague helped usher in the Renaissance, one of the most fertile times of innovation the world has ever seen.

In her book *War: How Conflict Shaped Us* historian Margaret MacMillan talks at insightful length about "war in our imaginations and our memories." She reminds us that the Greeks saw the seminal poet of war, Homer, as a "doctor of the soul." And she observes that "creating and consuming works of art," even during and following major conflicts, "can be an act of defiance as much as of hope." War, she says, can be a "vehicle for reconciliation."

Wars and pandemics will always be with us. We may wish our lives and our stories to be different than how they are, but that is heading toward ignorance and naiveté. As virologists have speculated, there are more viruses in our body than there are stars in the universe. That is a helluva lot of viruses. Fortunately for us – and the relentless powers of evolution – there are only about 200 viruses that cause us significant damage.

On the personal scale, there are many examples throughout history of individuals surviving the unimaginable, forging their own path forward. The Italian Baroque painter Artemisia Gentileschi had an incredibly traumatic youth, and ultimately a distinguished adult life. While still in her teens, she was tortured by the court at her own rape trial, which was intended to verify her testimony against her rapist. She went on to become one of the most important 17th-century artists, with an international clientele. She is only now receiving the wide attention and respect that should have come to her much sooner.

Two paintings by Artemisia Gentileschi: *Self-Portrait as a Lute-Player* **and** *Judith Slaying Holofernes,* **which some consider a work of symbolic revenge against the system in which she lived.**

So, all of this is to say that we've gone through things like the current pandemic ... and much worse ... before, and we will again. Somehow (although sometimes just barely) we manage to survive. And sometimes, in the aftermath, we even flourish.

Sincerely, and Technologically, Yours

Perhaps because I have several email address (I've got different ones for different needs), and because I'm active on Instagram, and sometimes on Facebook and Twitter, I get assaulted by multitudinous items of e-junk every day.

"Flirt Live with SexyGirls on RussianWoomen. Now!"

"This 2-Second trick KILLS 20 years of Aging?!"

"LAST CHANCE – congratulations! You've won a trip to Bora-Bora …"

Sometimes the pitches are so ingenious that I'm tempted to open up the emails. Not so much for the "Get Your Majic Penis Extender!" posts, but I once got an mail that said "Greetings from Tom" and because I had been thinking about an old friend named Tom and how I hadn't spoken to him in years, I opened the email. And that's when I got poked in the eye with "Bust your fat and Boost Your Metabilism! Today!!" Ah well, no real harm done.

Technology – including language, the wheel, dental floss, and particle accelerators – has always been a metaphor for what humans think is important. At times we choose to fill our minds with tumultuous insignificance and at other times we use technology to ponder through tentative answers about our most fundamental questions. We often tell ourselves the same old stories, over and over again.

There are some who think the Internet is changing who we are as human beings. I disagree. Or, put another way, the Internet has changed us, but so has the printing press, electricity, and eyeglasses.

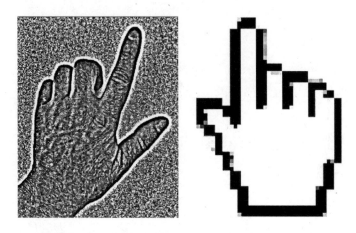

Our technologies change who we are, but just the parts that are easily changed. "We shape our tools and thereafter our tools shape us," said Marshall McLuhan. I think it is just as true to say: "Our tools shape us, but it is we who shape the tools." We adapt to our tools and technologies, and they adapt to us. But the human fundamentals that have taken a few million years to develop are not so easily transformed – fundamentals that include frivolous and infantile behaviors, as well as those that are imaginative and forward-looking.

You are immersed in, marinated by, the Internet. The digital world is the one you grew up with and that you now know instinctively. But we managed to get to this generation without computers. And previous generations managed to get by without the steam engine or the spinning jenny. Somehow we muddle through.

Just remember that the Internet is a tool – nothing more or less. It competes with or complements the natural world, but it does not replace it. "If you follow nature, you will not need technology," said Seneca, but of course he wrote those words with the technologies he had at hand – a lead stylus and a wax tablet, which he could erase and use again by wiping the beeswax surface smooth.

Sometimes I wonder about the people (or bots) that send me these junk emails and posts. Why do they do it? Do they care about clogging up my digital in-boxes, and those of billions of other people? Probably not.

Erase, wipe smooth, move on.

I've sent you many emails, texts, and links over the years. At times, I send you the following loving and affectionate note, here in its entirety: "L."

Because you are now heading off on your own, I want to send you a more loving and affectionate note: "LLLLLLLLLLLLLLLLL."

Make It Up as You Go Along

"My life would be a beautiful story come true, a story I would make up as I went along."

That's Simone de Beauvoir writing at the age of 50, in *Memoirs of a Dutiful Daughter*, about her 17-year-old self as she begins to study literature and languages at the Institut Sainte-Marie in Paris.

I'm not sure there have been many women more deliciously alive – more adventurous, inquisitive, strong, and passionate – than Simone de Beauvoir.

"I merrily defied convention and authority," she writes.

She goes dancing and reads voraciously and explores love and wonders about beauty. She demands the freedom to pursue her wishes and her passions. She is dutiful, as the title implies, but it is a duty bound to her own unique fascinations.

"I preferred to wonder about things than to understand them."

Although always thinking and always weighing options, she does not over-analyze, but rather follows the whims and the potential dangers of her restless and enthusiastic intellect. Understanding, she seems to say, can come later – for now, in her youth, it's more important to explore than to comprehend.

"There's only one spring-time in the year, I kept telling myself, and you're only young once: I mustn't fritter away any of my youthful spring-times."

She has that rare ability to both see herself in the world (caught within the rush and tumult of time) and to see herself in her own skin

and in her own unique moments (able to slow down the rush and tumult of time so that she captures the laughter, talk, and caresses most alive to her).

"I was reading Mauriac's *Good-Bye to Adolescence*; I was learning long languid passages of it by heart and I would recite them to myself in the streets."

From François Mauriac's book of poems, *Good-Bye to Adolescence*. While you're in the midst of spring-time, you should take advantage of the fruits the season offers.

Throughout her life, she was always able to capture the passions of others – of François Mauriac, of Jean-Paul Sartre, of Nelson Algren – and bend them to her own desires and needs. She was fascinated by many people, and many people were fascinated by her.

Even when she oscillated between depression and joy, between despair and confidence, as we all do, she always found a way toward work and pleasure and strength. "I loved life passionately," she said about her later teen years. And she would make resolutions to herself: "Be loved, be admired, be necessary, be somebody."

Simone de Beauvoir created the story of her life as she went along. And the foundation of this creation was a strong sense of wanting to live courageously, and with commitment and passion. As she heads off to college she says: "I was moving forwards, under an open sky, across the reality of life. The future was no longer just an impossible dream: I was touching it now."

All Advice is Useless

Over the years I have been given lots of advice and I have also sought out lots of advice – from poets, philosophers, scientists, entrepreneurs, family members, and many others.

And this is a sort of advice-book, which demonstrates (I guess) that I too am involved in the advice game.

Some of the snippets of advice that I've absorbed have had value – I've made use of various sorts of wisdom to get me through the day, or to provide some support when it was needed. I hope that some of the advice that I'm presenting here will have value to you.

If I had to boil down the observations I have for you into just a statement or two (trimming, distilling, reducing, rendering), I would say that the main thing you should try to do is figure out, over the course of your life, how you fit into the larger picture.

Ask yourself some questions. Don't assume that you'll always find the right answer immediately, and don't assume that the answer will stay the same over the years. As we get older (yikes, I'm really beginning to sound old here...) the questions we have and the answers we receive change. The fundamental questions we have in our teen years and in our thirties and in our sixties are always morphing – they get more complex, perhaps more contextual, and perhaps even more profound. So too with the answers.

Ask some questions about the larger world. Keep asking yourself "why?" Why does there seem to be a core of self-perpetuating ignorance and stupidity present in many people and in so many institutions? Why is there always a sense of freshness, newness, and optimism that is always bursting into life – in children and in people who want to discover more, and in the wonderments that seem always to present themselves for our appreciation?

Ask some questions about how you and the world are connected. These sorts of questions will keep you going until your final breaths!

Socrates, the foundation of so much of the way we see the world, was not shy or meek when he said: "The unexamined life is not worth living." Many, many people over the millennia have restated this wisdom, and have embroidered upon it. But the base of this statement is clear. Socrates does not suggest you'll come up with definitive answers. He does not say that you should seek happiness or even assume that you'll find wisdom. He certainly does not say that you should be reading advice books. He simply says to examine your life, and that will provide some worth.

Overlapping hearts from one of the many hand-made cards you've given me over the years. I've kept every one.

I would say that at this point in your life, as you head off toward real independence, most advice is useless – because you already have the basis for all questions and doubt and wonder and knowledge within you.

As a father speaking to his daughter, I look back to Socrates and I look forward to you.

And as a father, I articulate my love for you and at the same time encourage your unique freedom, so that you can find your own wisdom wherever you seek it, and your own paths, wherever they may lead.

To love and let go.

Acknowledgements

Thanks to the following, who supported this project, influenced the ideas within these pages, or read and commented on various drafts: Lida Alirezaei, David Bale, Pat Baranek, Lois Bennett, Maggie Berg, Robyn Buchman, Lauralee Edgell, Howard Ginsburg, LeeAnn Janissen, Barb Leckie, Neil Little, Carl Muñana, Bridget O'Brien, Colleen O'Brien, Sheilagh O'Connell, Siobhan O'Connell, Chris Osgood, Peter Paul, Rita M. Reichart, Cassandra Rodgers, Tia Sarkar, Bob Shantz, Zoë Share, Mary Stinson, Joel Westheimer, and Ruth Westheimer.

Special thanks to Rita Wuebbeler for suggesting the main title.

Ongoing thanks to Howard Aster, who has been supportive and encouraging throughout this and other bookish projects. And thanks to Rahim Piracha for his editorial and design wisdoms.

A couple of the ideas in this book have been explored in other words and for other purposes in my books *Cleopatra at the Breakfast Table: Why I Studied Latin With My Teenager and How I Discovered the Daughterland* and *A Perfect Offering: Personal Stories of Trauma and Transformation.*

Citation and Illustration References

Index

Italicized page numbers indicate illustrations.